PRAISE FOR *MEDIUM*

"Probing the confines of time, the textures of geographies and cultures, and our ability to address one another and really listen, Johanna Skibsrud offers multivocal monologues attuned to phantom voices. These poems speak and speak again, becoming various types of mediums: a means of tracing often silenced, forgotten, or mislaid lives; the very substance, the hard material of evanescent bodies transubstantiated into a kind of permanence; voices communicating between the imagined and the real. Whispering in our eye-ears, they pass no judgment. Instead they offer us their open word hands, so that we might take them."
—Oana Avasilichioaei, author of *Eight Track*

"The accumulation of voices in Skibsrud's *Medium* serves to reclassify individuality, offering a choral refuge and a devotion to a larger field of inquiry. Readers will delight and be haunted by the invocation of the 'divine feminine.'"
—Annie Guthrie, author of *The Good Dark*

"Sybil-like, Skibsrud uses each of her subject's *vidas* (lives) as springboards for creating the *cansos* (poems) that make up the wonder that is *Medium*. Each of these women's voices becomes audible, their bodies fully fleshed, their emotions and essence masterfully articulated. This collection presents an entirely novel means of actualizing the troubadour paradigm. It's a gift one can enjoy unwrapping for a long time, each time finding something new. To read these poems is to enter a world of beauty and meaning. What we have here is the work of an extraordinary poet."
—Beatriz Hausner, author of *She Who Lies Above*

PRAISE FOR
THE NOTHING THAT IS: ESSAYS ON ART, LITERATURE, AND BEING

"Skibsrud invites us to participate in the very human process of re-seeing and remaking the world; she challenges us to venture with her into the unknown, where experience and language empty themselves, then create themselves anew."
—Sam Ace, author of *I Want to Start by Saying*

"Skibsrud's work considers ideas as large as time and death and lingers gracefully on how literature knits with human life. Plenty of writers swimming among such big concepts have been lost at sea, but Skibsrud sails through with confidence."
—*BOMB Magazine*

"*The Nothing That Is* succeeds, primarily, as an argument for the potential of art and literature—and an invitation for readers to realize that potential for themselves."
—*Broken Pencil Magazine*

"*The Nothing That Is* signals Skibsrud's versatility as a poet and writer who is able to winnow and subvert theoretical concepts for ambitious reinvention."
—*Quill & Quire*

"Johanna Skibsrud has written a manifesto of liminal, reverberative space, as essential to our understanding of poetry and art, as to that of black holes and the Milky Way."
—Brandon Shimoda, author of *Hydra Medusa*

MEDIUM

Johanna Skibsrud

MEDIUM

Johanna Skibsrud

POEMS

Book*hug Press
Toronto 2024

Library and Archives Canada Cataloguing in Publication

Title: Medium : poems / Johanna Skibsrud.
Names: Skibsrud, Johanna, 1980– author.
Identifiers: Canadiana (print) 20230481434 | Canadiana (ebook) 20230481477
  ISBN 9781771668736 (softcover)
  ISBN 9781771668743 (EPUB)
  ISBN 9781771668750 (PDF)
Classification: LCC PS8587.K46 M43 2024 | DDC C811/.54—dc23

The production of this book was made possible through the generous assistance of the Canada Council for the Arts and the Ontario Arts Council. Book*hug Press also acknowledges the support of the Government of Canada through the Canada Book Fund and the Government of Ontario through the Ontario Book Publishing Tax Credit and the Ontario Book Fund.

Book*hug Press acknowledges that the land on which we operate is the traditional territory of many nations, including the Mississaugas of the Credit, the Anishnabeg, the Chippewa, the Haudenosaunee, and the Wendat peoples. We recognize the enduring presence of many diverse First Nations, Inuit, and Métis peoples, and are grateful for the opportunity to meet, work, and learn on this territory.

Book*hug Press

For Janet, Ellen, and Peggy,
For Kristin,
And for Olive and Sol

CONTENTS

PREFACE

This project began a decade ago, while I was pregnant with my first child. I kept thinking during that time, and afterward —through those first all-consuming years of parenthood, two miscarriages, and the birth of my second child — about the ways in which women have served as mediums throughout history, and of the ways they continue to serve. I thought of and looked again and again for guidance from the powerful women whose bodies, minds, and spirits have acted as conduits of knowledge and intuition; as points of convergence for the past, present, and the future; and as concrete points of channeling and accessing a way forward — or sideways, or otherwise.

It may be that every book is an effort to test the boundaries of the self: language imagined as a sort of bridge between the known and the unknown, between subjective perspective and whatever the subject is not. In extending these poems across vast breaches of language, experience, sensibility, and time, my hope is that they'll testify to distance as well as to desired or potential proximity. More than that, though, I hope they might lend shape to those aspects of experience we presume to be "unknowable," "unspeakable," or prohibitively "other," so that even distance and difference might be encountered not as a breach but as a connective element: one that joins us to one another, as well as to what we don't, and perhaps can never, understand.

The limits these poems evoke are real, in other words. But so, too, are the possibilities of lyric poetry understood in the broad sense suggested by the cultural historian Johan Huizinga "to include not only the lyrical genre as such but all moods expressive of rapture."

Of all possible modes of linguistic expression, the lyric, Huizinga writes, is "the farthest removed from logic" and can therefore be considered a close cousin to "music and dance." These poems were written in celebration of this ancient kinship. They are intended to evoke, and revel in, the indistinctions between body and spirit, sense and nonsense. They're intended to be read out loud; to be donned like masks. Also like masks, they're intended to be playful conduits for magic, and for the voices of others. They're intended to tell stories, drawing predominantly from the experiences of people now long gone, but they're also intended to operate in a prophetic mode. Specifically, my hope is that there remains room within the poems' structures for the reader (you) to bring about new ways of experiencing and understanding them. In keeping with the speaker's role as medium, I hope these poems may serve to amplify the voices of their readers and performers, while at the same time — in a choral, rather than a rhetorical, mode — asking: Who *is* speaking, really? And who isn't? Who, or what, is being addressed? Finally, what new possibilities or relations might potentially take form in the space of that address: in the space between "I" and "you," or between speech and silence?

At a certain point, while struggling to balance the lyric and narrative elements of this book, I was directed toward Lisa Robertson's *Anemones: A Simone Weil Project* ("If I Can't Dance" 2021) and her contemporary reimagining of the vida — the short biographical texts that once introduced and provided commentary on the manuscripts of troubadours. *Medium* employs this obsolete form as a way of embracing the tension between voice and text and emphasizing poetry as a mode of attention rather than of communication — a generative enactment of intimacy and exchange.

Like the vidas employed by the troubadours, the brief biographies I include in this collection are less interested in historical or narrative detail and more interested in elaborating the lived dimension of each poetic text. They include description and qualifying remarks about the subject of each poem: in each case, a specific human life the poems point to, perform aspects of, and imaginatively evoke, but can neither represent nor contain.

Early vidas sometimes constrained themselves to a sentence or two — the first describing the poet and the second describing the body of work. Later vidas, from the fourteenth century onward, developed into what Margarita Egan calls "portrait stories," and can be considered a literary genre in their own right. These later, more elaborate vidas tended to blend "literary" and "non-literary" references to the poet's life and oeuvre and to focus on the struggles poets underwent either securing patronage for their work or security in love. In my own experiments with the vida form, I've likewise tried to emphasize the connection between the literary and the non-literary: specifically, the ways that cultural, historical, and economic forces help to shape the possibility of the projection and reception of a single voice.

My hope is that many of the poems that follow will operate independently of their accompanying "portrait stories," or can be read and understood in connection with other stories — across continents and centuries. At the same time, each poem is an effort to explicitly acknowledge, and pay tribute to, the lives of the specific individuals that inspired them.

Linked to the mother goddess, Cybele — worshipped by the Greeks as the deity of bees and caves — the ancient "sybils" were prophets and seers. The first recorded mention of a sybil is by Heraclitus who, in the fifth century BCE, wrote of a "frenzied mouth uttering things not to be laughed at, unadorned and unperfumed" — of a voice that "reaches to a thousand years [...] by aid of the god."

THE SYBIL SPEAKS

A voice is an opening, nothing more. A hesitation
between breath and word, idea and form.

A hesitation that seizes, that takes hold. As the flickering
of a flame, a sudden gust of wind, a brief embrace.

They come. For centuries, they've come. In the name of
peace, of war, of love, and of bitterest revenge. I've been
entreated.

For centuries, heeded and ignored, flattered and defiled,
scolded and praised. I've been approached at every hour,
from every angle, and by every manner of men — of whom

I will say only this: there has been very little shame.

And yet, still, they come slowly, are careful not to look
me in the eye, and know enough to whisper as they beg for
directions to the entrance of hell.

And yet, still, they need a door. A madwoman. A way of
marking the distance between

my voice and theirs. Between language that speaks and
the sound

wind makes as it whistles through cracks in hollowed
stone. Between what exists — what *is* — and what...

> *War!* Fierce War! I say.

> I see the Tiber, the Euphrates,
> the Yangtze, the Nile —

> I see the Mekong, the Volga,
> the Gila, and the Mississippi River all
> running with blood!

Go ahead: Call it something. Give it a name.

That which glides like a wave that never breaks, or a
horizon that can never be drawn.

That which has no point of view; cannot therefore be
entered, let alone exited; let alone measured or claimed.

Still, they feed me on bulls from the field, razed corn, and
the blood of their own daughters, and sons.

Still, they need a door. An entrance, and permission to
enter. An exit, and the idea of return.

They need a finger to point with — and rage. They need a
body, and a hole in that body. They need to hear the wind
whip through my open jaw.

> Look! You, here!

> Lingering at the chipped rock
> of the open door.
> Afraid, like all the others.

Listen to the wind! And to the voices outside. To animals
in heat, gulls in flight, children laughing, or being born.

Smell the stench of meat on the altar. Of wood burning.
Of the dampness of grass after heavy rain.

Feel the pang of hunger, and the first tremors of love.

Taste salt and bread, fear and longing; blood. Water. Wine.

I cannot reveal anymore. I can only address you.

You, who have come. Like all the others have come.

A mystic from the fourteenth century, Lalleshwari, or Lal Ded — "grandmother" — wrote short imagistic vatsuns, or vakhs — a word deriving from the Sanskrit, "vachan," which means simply "voice," or "speech." Through her verses, Lalleshwari celebrated the possibilities of non-dualistic language and thinking in an effort to break down perceived boundaries between selfhood and the Divine.

I STOOD BEFORE MYSELF
AND REACHED OUT

I stood before myself and reached out to know myself
but each time my fingers closed around something or
someone else.

My skin was thin, but nevertheless it proved a barrier;
I could bring nothing closer.

No matter how hard I pressed, the thing I pressed against
pressed back.

Everything looked back at me with the face of another.

I felt hunted, alone — perhaps inexistent.

As brittle and wayward as a leaf, I blew and blew in little
circles inside myself, until at last I came to rest at my
own feet, unrecognizable.

So that it was only by chance that I picked myself up as if
I was another.

By chance I closed my fist around myself and turned to
dust in my hand.

The daughter of King Priam and Queen Hecuba of Troy, Cassandra, was favoured by Apollo and promised the power of prophecy in return for complying with his desires. In Aeschylus's version of the story, Cassandra accepts Apollo's proposal, then refuses to submit. In punishment, Apollo curses her, promising that though she'll still have the prophetic gifts he promised, she'll go unrecognized for them and never be believed. Unheeded, Cassandra would go on to accurately predict the fall of Troy, the death of Agamemnon, and her own demise.

I CAN'T EXPLAIN IT,
CAN SAY ONLY

I can't explain it, can say only it was

a gift, an offering, a simple exchange —
known for unknown thing.

> [The fire reaches the water's
> edge; the city burns.]

Can say: the future extended itself,

but as something to be   through,
exactly like the past.

> [The daughter's wrists already broken,
> my torch put out;
>
> my little axe already
> wrested from my hand...]

Can say only that if I *believed in an equation*
(future to the past, known to
unknown thing) I was well within my bounds.

[She'll be taken to the altar. He —

taunted and beaten.
Dragged through the streets.]

Yes. If I believed or if I did not, I was — given the parameters —

[The daughter murdered, and even
my lover,

my captor, slain...].

Everything just words now. Yours against mine.

I can say only it was never my intention nor my
nature to deceive,

and only natural, given the parameters,
to have imagined

an equation, a simple exchange. Only

natural to have imagined the future
like the past, a thing to be

moved through, given time; time a way
to move, to *be* moved.

           [And my own throat...yes,
           complicit. Open to the bone.]

I can say only the heart repeats itself,
chides endlessly:

           How, then, *if you knew?*

I can't explain it. Can say only the mind
tilts, trying; but there's nothing to

slide toward or lie against, nothing to
uphold.

In November 1953, a team of construction workers uncovered a buried cache of documents while making repairs to underground wires in the Jilin province of Northern China. The cache included personal letters, military files, and bank records that substantiated the mass rapes carried out during the Nanjing massacre, or "Rape of Nanjing," as well as the forced prostitution of up to 200,000 women — most from the Korean Peninsula — during the Second World War. The hidden cache (so large it might have "filled an entire truck") offered testimony of these atrocities, and many of the workers who uncovered the cache would have been separated from the exploited women by a single generation. Despite this relatively brief length of time, the retrieved documents were stuck together so tightly they formed a solid mass. Handed over to archivists in the early 1980s, they were released to the public in 2014. Most remain unreadable.

I REMEMBER THE *PING, PING*

i.

I remember the *ping, ping*
of my shovel as it struck —

the impact in
my elbows and neck.

Stand back, I said.

And knelt, and touched
the hard black shell beneath

a crust of dirt.

I remember the *scritch
scratch* of our shovels

and the sun beating overhead.

We threw our backs and shoulders
against it but at first it wasn't

clear how far the object extended and
for a long time there seemed to be

nothing to uncover.

ii.

When my grandmother was
still alive, she used to
get up sometimes

in the middle of the night
and stand by the window —
look out.

It would be dark outside.

It would always be raining.

Invisibly, the rain would be
falling outside, and yet

it would leave an impression,
a certain shape against the glass.

My grandmother's face, reflected
back at me, is always in any case

splintered in my memory, as though

peering at me through little drops
of light.

It was a sickness, my father said.

A certain, uncurable disease. We
must not mind her.

She used to stand there and look out.

Sometimes she would speak.

It was nonsense, my father said.
A made-up language.

Still, I remember I listened as if
the meaning could be

lifted somehow.

Marie Salomea Skłodowska-Curie (1867–1934) was a Polish-French scientist whose discovery of polonium and radium revolutionized science, led to innovative cancer treatments, and helped toward estimating the age of the earth. Along with her husband, physicist Pierre Curie, she was awarded her first Nobel Prize in 1903. Three years later, when Pierre was hit by a horse-drawn carriage as he stepped off the curb and died, the couple's eldest daughter, Irène, was nine years old and their younger daughter, Ève, was two. Marie dedicated herself to her research, as well as to the education of her daughters.

SOMETIMES, I TELL MY DAUGHTER, YOU MAY FEEL

"Sometimes," I tell my daughter, "you may feel
  one thing so strongly it seems it's the only true thing."

"But then the feeling splits into two, and you find
  there are other true things."

She holds onto my hand and doesn't look up.

"It's also possible, of course, to feel more than one thing.
  Or for a single feeling to break down steadily into other
  feelings over time."

She begins to cry. There's nothing more I can do. There
are, after all, only a very few hours in the day; they, at
least, do not divide endlessly.

I turn. She reaches after — .

"It's best to leave quickly," they
tell me.

"She *must* learn."

Life is heaped up. Just so much matter. But inside,
inside...

I imagine everything I've ever touched, everything I've
ever thought, everything that's ever brushed up against
my heart or mind, as little blue lights inside of my body,
invisible to the naked eye.

On the surface, most days are dull now. The work is
steady but fails to progress. Mornings are difficult. The
children peck at each other. It does not become any easier
to say goodbye.

And yet, at the same time, everything seems to be a
letting go.

"You are strong and brave, like Papa," I tell the
youngest one and pry her little hand from mine.

And turn. And pretend to be brave. Though most days,
frankly, I would prefer, rather than turning, to take her
back inside my body; would prefer

never leaving — never learning, never having to learn.

But it makes no sense — you can't go backward like that.
So I don't.

I push her out, instead. Steadily, I expel her.

It's painful, but at least the pain is pure. At least there's nothing beneath it, nothing otherwise. At least

it glows.

Hildegarde of Bingen (1098–1179) was a German writer, philosopher, botanist, composer, musician, and mystic. She is best known today for her music, which is still regularly performed and recorded, as well as for her leading role in founding the study of Germany's scientific natural history. Less well known is her Lingua Ignota, a twenty-three-letter alphabet she constructed for unknown purposes. In a letter received shortly before her death, a friend — perhaps fearing that whatever mystic secrets the language preserved, or was designed to transmit, would die with her — asked, beseechingly, "where, then, the voice of the unheard melody? And the voice of the unheard language?"

IN THE CHURCHYARD, THE SPECKLED BIRD

In the churchyard, the speckled bird. Its voice
a gift, a course of flight; word to named thing.

> AIGONZ! Inimois luzeia Inimois oir
> Inimois nascutil, moniz, osinz...
>
> Korzinthio, Runzgia,
> HOIL, fasinz, ceril...[1]

A bird dives for the worm, a moth to the flame. I have
beat my wings against the glass. Been

broken, mended. Drowned, and saved. I have been
burnt and scattered; been born, tossed. In every direction
upon the wind.

---

[1] From Hildegarde of Bingen's unknown language. Translation: "GOD!
Human eye Human ear Human nose, mouth, jaw... Prophet, Tongue, HEAD,
skull, brain..."

Yes, borne! AIGONZ!
Inimois luzeia Inimois oir Inimois
nascutil, moniz, osinz...

Day and night. Without the defect of ecstasy. Just: the
simple process of enumeration. Just — a record. The effort

of the mind and of the hand. To clarify the contents of the
body. To name everything, not as it should be, but as it is.

To be, and to name, not "I" — but each:

blind man, deaf man, dyspeptic, mute. To be, and to name,
the body as throat and thigh; as foot, sole, toe. To be
blood and urine, scab and blister. To be: pudendum, liver,
running sore.

To be earth; to be the first plowed field; to be
undergarment and sleeve; to be peddler and bishop,
cupbearer, spy.

This is not language, it is

       cap, mantle, knife. It is

       scythe and cauldron,
       battle-axe and wheel. It is

torch, cabinet, linen, sword. Bunghole, spigot, cellar,
flail. Spindle tree, laurel, bay leaf, rose....

It is incomplete. Flawed. Barely spoken. It is

34

fishermen without fish, shepherds without sheep,
sons — but no daughters.

It is song, transcription.

But no music. No words.

It is without article. Without duty, justice,
or truth. It is

that which is spoken. That which
cannot be repeated. The simple movement
of body and breath. It is

> Oneziz, pioranz,
> milizamiz, tirix...

> Veriszoil, scorinz,
> Kulzphazur, larchizin[2]

the mingling of sound and silence. Invented in the
moment of utterance. Knowledge that cannot be
abstracted from faith, or from desire. Desire that cannot
be abstracted from missing things.

Contents without system. Touch without imprint or promise.

Tongue, mouth, jaw.

2 Translation: "Door, key, image, threshold...
   Womb, heart, Ancestor, scribe..."

In part one of Aeschylus's *Oresteia* trilogy, Clytemnestra murders her husband, Agamemnon, after his triumphant return from the Trojan War. She welcomes him at first — wrapping him in cloth — then stabs him to death with a knife. The act is motivated by anger, both at being forced into marriage after Agamemnon murdered her first husband, and at the sacrifice of their daughter, Iphigenia, who was killed in order to secure Agamemnon's success in the war. Clytemnestra's actions have also been understood to be influenced by her alliance with Agamemnon's cousin and rival Aegisthus, as well as by the curse placed on Agamemnon's family, the House of Atreus, after the founder of that line fed his brother the flesh of his own children.

ENTER, KING

Enter, King.

Let me embrace you.

Let me extend, in offering,
this made thing, this single cloth.

You — who've met
good fortune, and a steady wind.

Who've raised hands in supplication
and triumph — who've raised

daughters, sons.

Tell me again it was the only choice.

Enter. Embrace me.

With your bare hands and in my sister's name,
the blood of our daughter still stinking on your skin.

Come, King. Tell me again it was a fair bargain,
and the only choice.

It is not a deception. I promised nothing — was
taken; was granted. My fate like my hands bound,
our daughter's blood already

latent, coursing through me, already
                    half-spilled —

Come. Leave your spear at the door, unprick
your ears — there is nothing to fear any

longer. All is familiar.
                    Listen!

That's the scratching of sumac branches
on the gate.

It's the bleating of sheep being shorn. It's
a distant bell.

Come. It is not a deception because
I promised nothing. Because —

there was no vow.

                    If, then, in your absence,
                    I fed the flame of fury;

if, then, in your absence, I

invited it into my bed.

If I plotted, fanned the flames,
if I burned. If I

wanted to burn —

it was not a deception because
there was no vow.

There was

a daughter. There was

a choice, made — .

Your prayer
raised

to an unanswering
wind.

I am not hungry — . Come. Let me
embrace you. Let me

wrap you in this single cloth.

Let me

plunge my hands into the fold, untie
the knot, unravel the weave — .

Let me fly, like loose thread, toward

you

who have asked for
and been granted protection;

you

who have made a fair bargain,
then more than paid the price;

you

whose ship has sailed — sped
home again on gentle winds;

you

whose bare hands
have raised hell with the blood

of daughters, sons — .

Come.

There is no way forward
save through this single,
open door.

Leave the girl in the yard;
she knows. How men come

willingly, are

indiscriminate; will sit at

any table, sup with voracious
appetite.

       Come.

         We've fed enough.

It was a choice, made — and as for
every made thing, an end.

Let me extend to you, in recompense,
the future fashioned by

your own hands.

It is here, among us. It is
          latent, granted. It is

          a body, it is a
          single cloth.

In 1826, one year before slavery was abolished in New York, Sojourner Truth, née Isabella Baumfree (1797–1883), was promised her freedom. When that promise was quickly retracted, Truth made up her mind to leave anyway. Taking her infant daughter with her and leaving her son, Peter, and another daughter behind, she walked away. One year later, when all New York slaves were emancipated, Truth learned that Peter — then only five years old — had been re-enslaved after being illegally sold to a man from Alabama. She became the first black woman to ever successfully challenge a white man within the American legal system and Peter was finally returned from the South. He lived with Truth in New York City until 1839 when, after a brush with the law, he was offered a job on a whaling ship in return for bail money and never seen again.

I GO DOWN TO THE DOCK

I go down to the dock
and watch the ships,

their great hulls
groaning, water

gushing out of
little holes in their
sides.

Everything goes up
and down, the
thick ropes

strained
against the pier.

I walk along and
listen to the screech
and groan of ropes

43

and hulls and

wonder how
they keep afloat
somehow.

There are certain
laws —. Everything
goes up and down.

You've got to keep
your eye on something

steady —

got to fix your
eye on it,

got to keep on
looking

and moving toward
that steady thing.

I walk along and
think of you — a little

speck in all that
emptiness, going

up and down.

I watch water gush
from little holes,

watch the thick
ropes

strained
against the pier.

There are certain
laws —

forgive me. I had to
keep that in sight; had to

keep going — even in
darkness, had to

feel my way.

Then the sun came up —
pointed its

finger at me.

You were just a
speck in the distance
by then. I had to

keep that in sight,
had to

keep going —.

Elizabeth Shaw Melville (1822–1906) was married to Herman Melville. She and her children were his copyists and it was Elizabeth who completed and edited the manuscript *Billy Budd* after Melville's death. As she transcribed, Elizabeth would leave room for punctuation marks, which Herman later inserted himself. On more than one occasion during her lifetime, Elizabeth tried to communicate the extent of the physical and emotional abuse she and her children suffered as a result of what Melville once called "the great art of telling the truth," but her pleas for help were either silenced or ignored. For many years, unrest in the Melville household was explained primarily through references to Elizabeth Melville's poor housekeeping skills.

I HAVE BEEN BUSY

I have been busy
and have not swept,

you must excuse it.

I have been

pressed, stacked, ready —
and by my faith,

a white page I
tore in two,

it was a pleasure,
a great art, and

to tell the truth
I have been
busy and make
no mistake. I should

have swept. Should have

beaten the rug; you must
excuse it. It is

to tell the truth a secret
I've kept and

a poor house; you understand,

the breath comes later
if it comes, and

the truth, no doubt.

The children see me

pressed and, by mistake,
thinking

they've turned their
heads, are

struck no doubt; you
must

excuse it. It is a
great art and

by my faith —
the only thing I can
keep —

a secret I've

torn in two. A

white page.

We don't know either Julian of Norwich's real name or what her life was like before she recorded her *Revelations of Divine Love* — the first known book to be written by a woman in the English language, in the 14th century. Some suspect she was a mother before taking her vows, and that during the plague years she may have lost one or more children. Though one of the most commonly quoted phrases from *The Revelations* is "All shall be well," these are not Julian's own words but instead words she attributes to God. A long section of the book records a lengthy argument with God through which Julian struggles to make sense of this teaching.

WE FEARED THE WOOD

i.

We feared the wood, we feared the road. We feared the
bread, we feared the water. We feared the pilgrim, we
feared the judge.

The house was marked. The windows and the door nailed
shut.

How I wanted to suffer. How I wanted to be nailed up.

ii.

Spring again, I went down to the river where
the ice still clung fast to the
reeds around the muddy edge.

I took a step and the ice crackled underfoot — gave way.
I took another. Water seeped into my boot.

There's no limit, I thought. To any of this.

The body, the river, the muddy edge....

Ice collects on the surface, is real, but it is also
just water.

The sky, then,
not a ceiling, not a door —.

iii.

I stepped back then and walked quickly

away from the river — my feet
squelching out a funny sort
of rhythm on the road.

How foolish, I thought, to have desired
pain, as though it might be something
new when it came.

Or something mine.

In her 1952 acceptance speech of the National Book Award for non-fiction, Rachel Carson said, "We have looked first at man with his vanities and greed and his problems of a day or a year; and then only, and from this biased point of view, we have looked outward at the earth he has inhabited so briefly and at the universe in which our earth is so minute a part. Yet these are the great realities, and against them we see our human problems in a different perspective. Perhaps if we reversed the telescope and looked at man down these long vistas, we should find less time and inclination to plan for our own destruction."

Carson died in 1964 at the age of fifty-six. Two years earlier the publication of *Silent Spring* sparked the global environment movement, as well as much controversy and personal attacks against what many saw as Carson's "hysterical" and ungrounded fear of commercial pesticides.

I SHOULD, AT LEAST,
MAKE THE SHORT TREK

I should, at least, make the short trek
up the rise,

find a view. Something
a little more sublime.

Instead, I go out to the yard —

clear a little space in the
dirt with my foot; watch

as a line of ants
makes its way beneath it,

without looking up, in
single file.

Fear, I think, is not an idea;

my foot hovers. Likewise —
devotion.

The ocean heaves with matter.

The ground is solid underfoot.

Even air is not invisible, no —
nothing just

drops away. Everything only

exists, and then exists again,
differently.

Even now, look — I am not an
idea. I am a foot, which hovers,

which threatens to descend.

Just moments before the United States House of Representatives voted in favor of reopening the government after a shutdown in 2013, house stenographer Dianne Reidy (1965–) interrupted proceedings with the following appeal: "Do not be deceived. God shall not be mocked. A House divided cannot stand." Reidy later claimed that the Holy Spirit had been urging her to speak out for several weeks, "waking me up in the middle of the night and preparing me (through my reluctance and doubt) to deliver a message in the House Chamber."

WE WERE TAUGHT
TO BE SEEN, THEN,

We were taught to be seen, then,
not heard. In any case, I was

deathly afraid of strangers. I learned
to listen; to love God. I could type

sixty-five words per minute by
the time that I was twelve. "A

quick study," my mother always
said. I went to school, did my

homework, played out back in the
yard. At night, sitting in front of the

blue of the TV screen, I prayed that
I would die. I remember: I could almost

hear the voice that called, almost see
the path of endless light. I'd climb up

the crab apple tree by the fence and pretend
that the sounds the other kids made were

the sounds of distant planets as they moved,
and sometimes collided, with one another

out there. Their language, in any case,
meant nothing. I could not understand

a single word. One year, I remember,
the tree became infested with worms.

I went back and forth all morning with
big kettles my mother heated on the stove,

then poured them, as instructed, and watched
as the fat bodies curled and turned black before

they dropped, one by one, from the
branch to the ground. I sat out, then,

shivering in the tree house my father had
built. Made a little square with my fingers
so that when I looked through them
all I could see was the sky.

Although it was hoped that Anne Boleyn (1501–1536) would soon provide King Henry VIII with a male heir, she gave birth instead to the future Queen Elizabeth I in 1533. After Elizabeth's birth, Boleyn suffered either two or three miscarriages and fell out of favour with the King. She gave birth to a stillborn son in January 1536 and a few months later was accused of adultery, incest, and plotting to murder the King. She was imprisoned in the Tower of London, tried by a kangaroo court, and executed.

I BEGIN TO LOATHE THE KING

I begin to loathe the King; cannot, I admit, even
look at him now without something

catching in my throat. If he touches me I hold my
breath and shut my eyes. If I

        pull at his hair or dig my fingers into
        the back of his neck I

pretend it is desire, though

        he and I both know.

I bite my lip — hard, but not hard enough. Something
stops me, though I'm certain now I'm not

afraid, and do not even think that I would bleed.

I screw my eyes shut, clench my fists, bite the soft flesh
behind his ear — it

surprises me. How much *give* there still is to flesh and
blood. And room — somehow — between us. Enough,
at least, to pretend.

Afterwards, I plunge my hands into my own reflection
and think of

other women's bodies. How soft, but in any case how

empty they become. I pull out a single grey hair, spot a
dead bird on the path.

Everything is a sign, I think; but I am never sure of what.

Except for you, Elizabeth, I would hardly believe that one
thing could touch another and become something else.

But you exist — are living proof. Though even proof, now,
Elizabeth, is not enough, and

                he and I both know.

I admit, I used to name them. Used to think of them as
whole, already "mine."

If I saw a dark-winged bird it meant one thing; if I saw
two it meant another.

But I would wait all day if I had to, to see that second
dark-winged bird. I thought that it was up to me; that all I
needed was to watch the sky.

Last time, when it happened, I didn't even
cry out. I lay in bed. The pain came and went.

All night long, while the King slept.

There was even, I admit, a certain pleasure in it — a small
revenge.

At dawn, I crouched over the pot. While the King slept. A
rush of blood; a sudden

warm relief. I looked. The light was still quite dim, but
there it was, I could see it — gleaming. All those

tiny, perfect bones.

Hypatia of Alexandria was born sometime between 350–370 and died in 415 CE. She was a Neoplatonic philosopher, mathematician, astronomer, teacher, and counsellor, eventually murdered by a Christian mob. Although we have no record of Hypatia's philosophical response to Aristotle's discussion of the indefinite term, "not-man" — which can be found in the fourth and fifth sections of *The Metaphysics* — the problem the term presents was explored in depth by Ammonius (third century CE) and Boethius (475–526?). It is quite possible that Hypatia — a scholar of both Plato and Aristotle — would also have questioned and enlarged the philosophical discussion surrounding this term.

The disclosure, against that sign, of an infinite set
of other possibilities: of every *thing* (save the one thing
it is "not") that can either be conceived of or imagined,
including non-existence.

To be "not-man" is to be this infinite set.

It is to be privative without refutation; at once

rock and bird. Knife, woman, fish hook, child.

Teresa of Ávila (1515–1582) was a Spanish mystic, writer, religious reformer, and spiritual guide. Her paternal grandfather had been a marrano, or converted Jew, at one point condemned by the Inquisition for returning to his Jewish faith. But Teresa was born a Christian and a noblewoman — her father having purchased a knighthood after securing success in the wool trade. Teresa was introduced to mystic writings and romance novels by her mother and, as a child, dreamed of running away to North Africa in order to martyr herself there. At the age of twenty, she entered a convent and, after struggling with doubt, achieved the powerful connection with God she desired. Her fellow nuns were sometimes obliged to sit on her, or tie her down, in order to keep her ecstatic and sometimes painful visions from quite literally carrying her away.

"LET THEM SLICE OFF OUR HEADS"

"Let them slice off our heads in the desert," I whispered.
"Let our eyes roll up toward the heavens; let our bodies
turn to dust and be blown in four directions from our
bones."

I packed two sandwiches and an extra pair of stockings —
took my brother along.

When my uncle found us in the marketplace and
delivered us back home, my mother shook her fist,
then knelt and sobbed into her sleeve.

We tend to imagine our lives as though they are in
themselves a limit rather than a tool or simple accessory,
like a knocker on a door.

I used to weep over the passion until my head ached and I
could no longer see.

71

My father's father was a Jew, condemned; my mother
desired nothing more than to lead a quiet, Christian life.

I hear loud noises in my head, which make it hard to
write this down.

Muktabai or Muktai (1279–1297) was a mystic who became a saint within the Wakari tradition, a branch of Vaishnavite Hinduism. Muktabai lived only eighteen years but in that time wrote forty-one abhangs — a form of devotional poetry dedicated to the Hindu god Vitthal, or Vithoba — and performed several miracles. While still a child, Changdev, or Changadeva, a mystic and yogi already famous for mastering the powers of all five elements and resurrecting the dead, was inspired by Muktai's wisdom. She and her four siblings were taken into Changdev's charge and Muktai became his spiritual guide.

ONE DAY, A DEAD MAN

One day, a dead man was brought to the temple when the
old man, Changdev, was not about. "Oh, I can raise him
from the dead," I said, "just let me try." I rushed to the
body and threw myself at its feet.

The wind blew at the branches of the trees overhead and
the man who'd carried the body laughed out loud.

"Come child!" his kind wife said. "See here; it's no use."

But I'd already placed my hand on the body: it stirred,
turned warm, exhaled hot breath.

The man who'd carried the body cried out, so that
my brothers heard and ran from the house.

They stood by the fence and gaped while I
vomited onto my feet and the kind wife
clutched at her head and prayed.

Then Changdev himself came tapping across the yard.

"It was an accident," the man who'd carried the body said.

"It was a miracle," his wife and my brothers replied.

I looked back and forth between them and was afraid because I didn't know if what I'd done was good or bad.

Or — from the look on old Changdev's face — who could tell.

Annie Easley (1933–2011) was a mathematician and rocket scientist who began her career as a "human computer," performing complicated calculations for researchers in longhand. Despite the discrimination she faced as one of only four African American employees at her first lab, she continued to advance her career and paved the way for future generations of women working in the fields of science and technology. Among her many pioneering achievements, she developed code used to research alternative power and energy-conversion systems and contributed to NASA's Centaur rocket program—which laid the foundation for the Apollo moon landings.

WE WERE COMPUTERS, OFFICIALLY

We were computers, officially,
before there were machines.

Then — when the machines came —
we were "technicians."

When the men came we were
"ladies," "girls."

On weekends, we drove down to
the Cape to watch the Delta rockets
and the Centaurs fly.

We bought peanuts and popcorn.

There was always a crowd.

Later, I read about the real centaurs —
the ones we named the rocket for.

About how they got stuck between two
worlds and were often angry because of it.

They didn't seem to belong.

A lot of people don't know this,
but there were female centaurs, too.

I saw a picture of them, once.

Two female centaurs, one of them
with her face rubbed out.

That's just history, I thought,
looking at the rubbed-out space
where her face should have been.

Winter, I'd go out with the ski club,
glide down the slopes —

pretend I was flying or coming in
for a landing on the surface of the moon.

I'd look at all the little stunted trees
covered with snow and squint my eyes
so I wouldn't recognize the familiar
shapes of houses or buildings or roads.

I'd sail right past them — watch the lights
blink on at the lodge, and in town
and think of them like little stars.

You have to see things like that, from a distance,
the way a computer does — a machine.

You have to trust that the answers are
still coming, though you can't see how
they're being worked out —

that the problems have all been broken up
into little bits and become invisible, or at least

temporarily unseen.

Franca Rame (1929–2013) was an Italian actress and playwright who, born into a theatrical family that could trace their roots back to commedia dell'arte days, made her first appearance onstage at the age of only eight weeks old. Together with her husband, Dario Fo, Rame wrote and starred in countless productions performed to sold-out audiences in union halls and sports stadiums. The shows sought to entertain, raise awareness about political and social issues, and foster a sense of solidarity among the political left. In 1997, Fo accepted the Nobel Prize in Literature. He accepted it on behalf of himself and his wife, who — he emphasized — was an inextricable and elemental force within everything he wrote.

WHAT LUCK TO FIND MYSELF

What luck to find myself
like this, lit up, a single

speck at the end of a
long and narrow beam.

What luck to be at least
briefly illuminated —

a mote of dust, a
coagulate — caught; lit up.

To find myself "at the end";
no, to *be* that end, a

particular body — a mouth,
a way of opening.

What luck! To bite down and find

there really is something out there
to *sink one's teeth into.*

What luck — to see, or
begin to see, in perfect darkness

the becoming of teeth and lips,

the glare of eyeglasses....

To hear, in silence, the becoming of
a laugh, a shout.

To reach out and grasp,

or begin to,
the becoming of something

to seize
or be held by.

                    It has to be this way.

                    You have to invent
                    absolutely everything.

                    You have to dream it all up,
                    make it real.

                    You have to let your hand
                    hit on something when it

reaches out, you have to
give your words

something to catch against.

According to Greek legend, Helen of Troy's extraordinary beauty was the indirect cause of the Trojan War. She was the daughter of Zeus either by Leda or by Nemesis. In some versions of her story, Zeus appears to Leda in the form of a swan and either rapes or seduces her in this form. An egg is the result of this union and when it hatches Helen is born — along with her twin sister, Clytemnestra, and brothers, Castor and Polydeuces. In one version, Helen is eventually hanged by Polyxo, the queen of Rhodes, in order to avenge the death of her husband, killed in the Trojan War. In another version, Helen and Paris wash up on the shores of Egypt and Helen is captured and held there by King Proteus. In this version, the Helen that goes on to Troy is a phantom version of the real Helen who remains in Egypt and is only later retrieved by Menalaus, after the war.

IT WAS NOT ME

It was not me, it was a shadow.

Simple, immaculate — generating nothing.

It was a riddle — a little knot of
feeling, which took hold, took shape —

took wing. In the uncertain flutter of

my father's heart as it pounded itself into
the shape of a bird.

As it beat itself; as the skin puckered,
as it became empty-boned, feathered;

As its brain grew small and light, driven
by its single goal.

Just imagine. All that confusion of
      limbs and senses,

duty and desire — .

Imagine all that blood — that
shape-shifting. A mixing of

coincidence with the inevitable, hatred
with devotion.

What *is it,* I wonder,

to face something like that?

What is it to be faced?

This essential ambidextrousness
at the heart of both

nature and fate that would have us,
on the one hand, soaring — flightless —

outside of ourselves (peering back,
as from a reflection on water or glass) and,

on the other, contained like the meat of
a nut in its shell.

Which would have us always torn —

perceiving in ourselves a trembling, perfect
beauty we can never quite bear.

Well, I cannot bear it for you any longer, you must
bear yourself. Must —

                                    please; I beg you —

conduct yourself, your wars, without me,
if you can. Let me remain here, on this quiet shore.

I will wake every morning, I will wash. I will

feel in the cool weight of the water
poured on my temples, my neck, and
over the backs of my hands, the reduction of being

to a simple juxtaposition. As if the skin was
a barrier, a limit — and therefore

a point from which to imagine an origin,
an end.

I had a dream, once, I remember, that I had
wholly human bones.

And that my bones were hung by a rope —
dangled, for all to see. Disjointed.

I had a dream that my bones were
wholly human bones and

buried in the dirt. That they were ground
after many long years into a fine dust

and became sediment at the bottom of a
mountain stream.

I had a dream that I was a deer that
came one day and drank from that stream.

That I was quenched by the water that
rushed over the pulverized dust of my
bones.

What, I wonder,
is it to know,

or to want
to know,

if my mother *desired* my father? If she
was properly seduced? If her heart beat
like a little bird's the way mine did,
when young?

The world is

propelled by such beating, propelled —

by the mad beauty and single-mindedness
of youth in love.

By that...insensible yearning for the end
to meet with and once again
become the beginning.

For there to be no longer any question,
but instead only

a collision, a merging. A running
up against the boundaries of the species —

a ripple of something like disbelief

resulting in an exceptional
confusion over the

order of things.

Do you see —

                    now?

There never was any plot. Never any
causal structure. And it was not me

you loved. It was a shadow. It was
a riddle. A momentum of

fury and longing, a swirl of blood.

A divine logic compelled

by the insistent hammering of
animal hearts into

approximate form.

No, it was not for me you fought
and destroyed your

cities. It was... for this —
this simple, though nearly unutterable

wish for flight, and human bones.

It was for this — this impossible
riddle. Which saw itself

lifted — carried off; which departed
from itself and was returned.

                              Enough now!

                    Go!

I cannot bear you any longer.... But I can

          salute you. I can forgive you,
          and remain —

          yours.   Truly.

Still reveling in your solicitations,
still feeling the blood heat up
inside my veins. Still resting—

assured of the divinity of my body,
which is also yours. Still

touching everything.

Shakuntala Devi (1929–2013) was a writer, mathematician, astrologist, and politician whose extraordinary talent for mental computation earned her a place in the 1982 edition of *The Guinness Book of World Records*. Born in Bangalore, India, she first demonstrated her ability to memorize and compute large sums when her father — a magician and lion tamer — taught her a card trick at the age of three. She toured the world exhibiting her skill and authored many books including *The Book of Numbers*, *Astrology for You*, *Puzzles to Puzzle You* (from which some excerpts included in this poem were taken), and *The World of Homosexuality* (considered India's first academic study on the subject).

A BIRD IS THE SUM
OF ITS FEATHERS

A bird is the sum of its feathers, a necklace its pearls.

Everything exists because it can be counted; there is no
mystery in this, only questions, only certain choices to be
made.

Two identical trains begin at the equator and travel
around the world in opposite directions.

A little girl sells oranges every day, from door to door.

The distance between one thing and another can be
counted. The probability of one thing occurring over
another can be counted. The likelihood of attaining

material advantage is based on material means and
can be counted.

The possibility of sound sleep, good food, the gain of
clothing and ornament exists, and can be properly stated;

likewise, the possibility of unforeseen obstacles, heavy
expenditures, and criticism from friends.

The sun pulls upon the planets.

Mars is in transit, Mercury and Jupiter are in transit.

The north latitude of Agra and the east longitude of
Chittagong can be stated.

The minor sub periods of the sun and the minor sub
periods of Jupiter and the moon can be stated.

The risk of disease, injury, and sudden death is
enumerable; it can be counted. Likewise, the risk of

insolvency, repudiation, and falling in love.

Desire exists because everything is a risk and can
therefore be counted.

Two people passing beneath a eucalyptus tree move
toward one another with opposite intentions.
Two people, moving toward one another beneath a
eucalyptus tree, travel at relative speeds on parallel

paths, with opposite intentions. The point at which
they draw nearest to one another is precise,

and can be properly stated. Likewise, the moment
at which — drawing near to one another — they

fail to intersect. Desire pulls upon the body. The
future pulls upon the present, which pulls upon the past.

Two events taking place at a distance of either space
or time exist in a relation that is precise, and can be

counted. There is no mystery in this. Only questions.
Only certain choices to be made.

Grand Duchess Anastasia Nikolaevna (1901–1918) was the daughter of Russia's last czar, Nicholas II. She and her family were murdered in the Bolshevik uprising of July 17, 1918, but a rumour persisted that she alone had managed to escape. In the ensuing years, numerous women came forward claiming to be the murdered princess. The most credible was a nameless woman who, in 1920, attempted suicide by jumping off a bridge in Berlin. She was rescued and delivered to Dalldorf Asylum where another patient, Clara Peuthert, began to suspect that "Madame Unknown"—who had been assigned the name Anna Anderson—was in fact Anastasia Romanov.

Peuthert urged high-ranking Russian expats to meet Anna in order to confirm her suspicion, but Anna neither cooperated with nor encouraged these meetings. She often hid under the sheets when visitors arrived, angrily berating them, or refusing to answer their questions. Occasionally, memories surfaced for Anna that seemed to confirm the connection Peuthert had made, and she often seemed to recognize the faces of the people in the photographs she was shown. Still, Romanov relatives and acquaintances remained divided over whether or not Anna Anderson was the true Anastasia. A legal case that lasted more than thirty years came, at last, to an indefinite conclusion.

MEMORY IS A BLAZING THING

Memory is a blazing thing,
impossible to get too near.

It doesn't wish to
preserve anything, but instead

to consume, even to
extinguish itself.

And yet, looked at
from a distance —

        the sound of horses,
        of voices in the
        yard.

        The softness of
        crushed velvet, the
        scent of boiled
        tea —

Certain objects may begin to appear.

Illuminated by swift, uncertain
light —

> A door ajar. A hand
> pushed in. A face —
>
> blurred first by dark
> and then by cold.

Memory is the desire for
illumination. It's —

> Breath. A grey fog.
>
> A pressure on the
> throat.
>
> WHO DO YOU
> THINK I AM?

An animal with no skin, which wants
to crawl inside your bed. Which wants to

press itself against you, wants to
warm itself — and be warmed.

Except that there's
nothing to press against. Only...

We used to sail our
boats together on
the pond. Mine
never tipped. Or
when it did, it
always righted. The
sun came down in
streams; my hat was
tight; there was an
uncle

tapping his cane
along the path.

Does he see me
coming?

Does he recognize
me, now?

Hat pushed back,
hot-cheeked, flying
down the lane.

It's me, Uncle!

A collision of
colour and smell.

*Ha ha! You little
scallywag!*

                    Ha   ha   ha!

Memory is a boat that leaks.

A deaf man with everybody's
secrets to tell. Do not

give him an inch.

                    Ha!

                    Ha   ha

                            ha!

The boat will leak. The deaf
man will always betray you.

Now, the little cat leaps onto the bed.

It wants to settle, wants to curl up at
your feet, but it has no skin — can't
contain or warm you.

Memory is a stone to suck;

to turn and turn upon the tongue.

It's a nut too hard to crack. It's
a simple line. A jagged

cut across the sky.

Annie Fratellini (1932–1997) was born into a famous family of clowns. Granddaughter to Paul Fratellini of the Fratellini brothers — one of the most celebrated clown acts in circus history — the Fratellini family could trace their circus origins back to Enrico Gaspero (Gustave) Fratellini who fled a career as a soldier and then as a doctor to become a circus acrobat. Annie Fratellini performed the role of the slapstick "Auguste" — the first woman ever to do so — to her husband's "White Face." Her clown persona was rebelliously playful. She wore a large overcoat, a bowler hat, oversized shoes, and the red nose made iconic by her Uncle Albert. Because both her costume and character were deliberately androgynous, she was often asked if her clown was male or female, a question to which she would respond, "clowns have no gender!"

I MUST FIND MY HAT, MUST

I must find my hat, must

blow my nose, dust off
my bottom.

Look. The world is a
small ball, which can

be picked up, like this —

tossed back and forth.

It's not a trick, see? It's
a certain risk I'm taking.

Let me try it again; hold

onto my hat this time; find

my ball, my clarinet —
and blow.

It's not a trick. The spirit
resists — and yet

the body presses back
exceptionally

hard against the soul.

Let me try it again; always
the hat that goes — no matter.

Look.

The spirit — pressed to so
fine a point — resists,

leaks out, makes
noise.

It wants to travel. Wants
to be shot from

the inside of a cannon —

or pulled,

like an endless ribbon,
from a sleeve.

It's not a trick. Let me find
my hat; look.

Gravity is definite, clothing
cumbersome, shoes

ten sizes too large.

Henrietta Lacks (1920–1951), better known to science as "HeLa," was an African-American tobacco farmer from Roanoke, Virginia who was treated for cervical cancer at Johns Hopkins University in 1951. Although Lacks died from the disease later that year, leaving behind five children, her cells were preserved without either her or her family's knowledge or consent. HeLa cells have been copiously reproduced for medical study ever since. If laid end to end, it is estimated that they would wrap around the earth at least three times. HeLa cells have been flown to the moon, been inside nuclear bombs, and have in some way aided most of the major medical breakthroughs of the last century, including the development of chemotherapy and vaccines against polio and Covid-19. After a lengthy struggle, the surviving family of Henrietta Lacks reached an historic settlement with the multi-billion-dollar biotech company, Thermo Fisher Scientific, in August 2023.

TIME EXISTS, IT DOES NOT FLOW BACKWARD

Time exists. It does not flow backward. I
put on my jacket and shoes and walk outside.

My jacket — the shoes — the street — are real.

The direction I'm walking in is real.

My body is real. It does not flow backwards.

My shoes ring out like little dull bells on the street.

The sound they make is real — and the pain
in my hip.

I sit up; I put my hand on my heart. Listen:

My heart beats. My brain ticks like a clock.

I do not want to die.

I put on my jacket, my shoes — they are real.

I walk three or four times around the earth
in a single direction. The direction is real —

but the pain follows. I can't outpace it.

I course through the bloodstream of a rat. I
crawl inside of a nuclear bomb. I beat my

fists inside its empty shell and pray to God to
restore my faith in God.

I reach for my jacket and shoes and climb into
my spaceship.

The pain follows.

I check the controls — watch all the little
blinking lights — then close the hatch and

begin to count backward, from ten.

Everything shakes, then goes dark.

I do not feel afraid. Even my heart has stopped
pounding.

I float for a while up there in zero gravity and wait for the
pain to catch up.

There may be a slight lag, I think, but I'm sure that it will follow.

I look down at the earth and already it looks faraway and very small.

It would be nothing to wrap myself around it, even three or four times.

"Hello down there!" I say.

My breath fogs up the glass inside my helmet, which makes it difficult to see.

"Hello!"

My voice is muffled-sounding but I have the feeling it's still being

broadcast somehow.

Mary Mallon (1869–1938), better known as "Typhoid Mary," immigrated to the United States from Ireland at the age of fifteen. She worked as a cook for well-to-do families, often serving her signature dish, Peach Melba. After several members of the families that employed her died of typhoid, Mary underwent extensive testing. Though she exhibited no symptoms herself, it was finally concluded that Mary was a carrier of the disease and therefore directly responsible for the victims' deaths. These findings marked a turning point for researchers and immunologists, but Mary herself never accepted them.

Even after her release from quarantine on the condition that she never work as a cook again, Mary returned to her accustomed employment and her signature dish. The recipe, uncooked and served cold, quickly and easily transmitted bacteria. When more deaths were linked to Typhoid Mary, she was detained again — this time for good. Still healthy, and believing herself innocent, Mary Mallon spent the rest of her life in quarantine on North Brother Island, a small island in New York's East River.

DON'T TOUCH ME

Don't touch me. Don't ask me to explain. Look. I am an
honest woman. I am

healthy, strong, and every penny I have, I've earned.

                                        Don't touch me.

I come recommended. Don't ask me to explain. It kills
them every day in the slums.

                        Did you know that?

The Lord spoke. He said: I will send the pestilence
among you. But he didn't say how and said nothing of

exempting the residents of Fifth Avenue, or of Oyster
Bay.
                                        Don't touch me.

It kills them every day in the slums, but I am not

one of them. I am healthy, hardworking, clean. I come
recommended.

Don't *touch* me.

Whatsoever plague, whatsoever sickness there be...

We used to go down to the garden; used to watch the
souls of dead folk hop about like rabbits at the edge of the
lawn. They were amongst us. We did not think we were

too high and mighty, then.... And when they knocked on
the door, we opened it. And we were not surprised to see
only darkness there.

We were afraid — yes, *sore* afraid. But we did not think
we should be otherwise.

And if anyone died, we raced to place the hands of the
dead on our skin. Because —

we were innocent. Because we were
innocent and alive and God-fearing. Because we
prayed mightily, using simple words. And never once

questioned why our prayers went continually
unanswered. Which they did.

Don't touch me.

It's a simple recipe — and good. I am no murderess.

Tiresias was the blind prophet of Apollo who could see into the future and interpret the movement and language of birds. He is said to have spent seven years as a woman — a punishment for having attempted to separate a pair of copulating snakes. Sources are divided on how the "curse" was reversed and Tiresias finally regained his masculinity. Either it was simply by sighting a second pair of copulating snakes or it was through the act of destroying the snakes that Tiresias became a man again.

After the transformation, another story tells of how Zeus and Hera consulted Tiresias in order to settle a debate they were having over which of them enjoyed more pleasure in bed. When Tiresias replied that a man enjoys one tenth what a woman enjoys, he was blinded by Zeus for the offence. It was either as a further curse or as a recompense for physical blindness that Tiresias was granted the gift of prophecy.

"OF TEN PARTS, MAN ENJOYS…"

"Of ten parts, man enjoys
only one" — true. But I

did not mean
to suggest by this that
the female part was either

"more" or "better."

I meant only to point,
as usual, to

the unindexical;

meant only to question

the blind violence
wreaked upon

conjoinings; to defy
the categorical

parsing of personhood
and fortune;

to say:

nothing changed, nothing was
transformed. I was only

ever this, unnumbered body,
this

androgynous mind.

Rome burns. And burns.
And burns.

I cannot see the shape

the smoke takes,
but its inconstant form is

clearly described by my
own

inscrutable longings. I
reach out, have my

eyes plucked out.

I ask for simple signs.
I watch the sky.

The flight of birds is
characterless, I find,

but it is

bodied and distinct.

I cannot see, cannot

know each one,
but I can

detect, at least —
the movement

and necessary relation,
therefore,

between things that
travel, together, in a
sustained direction.

I know to keep

my hands outstretched —
to feel my way — to

watch the sky. I know

to stumble when I
meet something

difficult along the path.
And not to
call it a snake,

and to leave it uncleaved.

I know at least to call upon

the dead, and be roused
to anger when they do not

attend us.

Norma McCorvey (1947–2017) was better known as "Jane Roe," the plaintiff in the 1973 Roe v. Wade case that resulted in the United States Supreme Court ruling that it was unconstitutional for individual states to prohibit abortions. Battered and poverty-stricken, McCorvey was vulnerable to what she later claimed was undo pressure by pro-choice activists and lawyers to pursue the case. She emphasized her ambivalence about both the court ruling and her personal decisions at the time and, after converting to Catholicism, denounced both and became a vocal supporter of the pro-life movement. At the end of her life, however, in what became known as her "death bed confession," McCorvey admitted to having received monetary compensation for her support of the pro-life side and alleged that her support had never been sincere.

I AM A WOMAN
(BALLAD OF JANE ROE)

I am a woman. I am not the law. I am a woman. I am not
the law. I am a woman. I am a woman. I am not the law. I
am a. Child. I am a not the law. I wanted a. Woman. A
child. I am not the law. I wanted. A child. I am not the
law. A child. I wanted a child. I wasn't. I wanted. A
thing. I wasn't. I wasn't wanted. I was a woman. A thing.
And not a child. I was — the law. No — not the law. A
child. A thing. I am a woman and *not* the law. I am a
child. A woman. I am *not. Not. I am not.* Not wanted. I
wasn't. I didn't. I didn't want. *That thing.* Inside me. I am
a woman. I am not the law. I am not. Not the law. Inside
me. I am. Child. I am a woman. I am. Not the law. Not
the law.

Brunhilde Pomsel (1911–2017) spent three years working as the confidante and secretary for Joseph Goebbels up until May 1, 1945, when — shortly before Nazi Germany surrendered — he and his wife, Magda, poisoned themselves and their six children. Until her death at the age of 106 Ms. Pomsel maintained she was ignorant as to the extent of the Nazi's crimes. "Really," she claimed, "I didn't do anything other than type in Goebbel's office."

The 2016 documentary, *A German Life*, records Pomsel's commentary on her everyday life and career, including references to her childhood friend, Eva Roventhal, and the German surrender to Allied forces in May 1945.

EVERYTHING WAS STILL QUITE ALL RIGHT

Everything was still quite all right —
whether it was good or bad.

There were still well-dressed people,
friendly people.

Eva was there; everything was *all right.*

Whether it was good or bad. You had to
stand somewhere.

Eva, I remember, was waiting outside.
You had to

give them your name, your age,
and ten marks.

Ten marks! I remember. But still
I signed. What was the difference?

Oh God, I was superficial back then.

Politics? I said. Why should I?

Everything was still quite all right.

Whether it was good or bad.

The facts were proof enough.

Politics, I said? What for?

Of course, I had no idea.

I'm a woman; he didn't even try to convince me.

And what was the difference?

My God. Just to think of it. Eva was
gone. Eva had moved away by then.

Politics? I said.

For me, life went on.
Everything was still quite all right.

Eva! I said. I must come to
visit you.

I'm not quite sure how to put this.

It's better if you don't come, she said.

Oh God, I was frivolous, superficial at the time.

I was given a position. Whether it was
good or bad.

What for? I said. Then we all sat like
animals. We'd saved a little white flag.

Yes, I'm missing Eva Roventhal, I said.
He didn't even

try to convince me. My God,
just to think of it.

Politics? I said. To what end?

I'm not
quite sure how to put this.

Eva! I said.

Deceased.

That's all you could find out.

Rābi'a of Basra was an eighth-century Sufi mystic devoted to the doctrine of *ishq-e-haqeeq,* or divine love. It is said that Rābi'a of Basra, born into poverty, was enslaved, then freed by her master when he saw her praying in a field encircled in a holy light. She performed miracles and a significant body of poetry is attributed to her, though she left no written record.

THERE IS NO REASON

There is no reason for sun, or sea, cloud, or leaf.

No reason for dogwood, oak, elm, maple, seed,
or wind.

No reason for rain. For earth. For potato bugs, or eyeless
worms. No reason for frost or snow, for first thaw, for
snowdrops, or crocuses.

There is no reason that anything should emerge from the
earth — or return to it again.

No reason that things should be lost. Buttons, ships,
coins, words. Or found again.

There is no reason for *this* particular beam of light to
settle at *this* particular angle on *this* particular stone.

There is no reason for ragweed, milkweed, dandelion,
thistle; for jackdaw, eiderduck, house sparrow,
crow.

There is no reason for dinner jackets or umbrellas;
for boots or mufflers, pockets, or rings.

There is no reason for thimbles, levers, axles, screws;
for mixing bowls, whisks, or wooden spoons.

There is no reason that beasts should suffer or that a hop
or a fig should dry on the vine. There is no reason a house

should burn or that a man should either drown or grow

old. There is no reason to pray, no reason to suffer, no
reason to be faithful, merciful, prudent

or kind. There is no reason.

You may be born dead or dumb, weak, or poor. You may
be born temperate, chaste, diligent, just —

but for no reason. You may be a slave, as I was a slave.

For no reason. You may pray — and be touched by God —
and glow like a flame. For no reason. You may be

set free as I was set free. And discover that
freedom exists — a simple fact — which, like God,

can be denied. For no reason.

Eliza Grace Symonds (1809–1897) was the wife of Alexander Melville Bell, the creator of "visible speech" — a technique that helped the deaf learn to speak — and the mother of Alexander Graham Bell. Although deaf, Eliza Symonds became an accomplished musician and was so attuned to the vibrations around her she claimed to be able to feel the sound made by a human voice through her skull. It is for this reason that she preferred her son, Alexander, to press his lips to her forehead rather than speak through an ear trumpet. Her son's later interest in the palpable qualities of sound and its transmission across space and time was no doubt influenced by these early conversations with his mother.

PUT DOWN YOUR TRUMPET

Put down your trumpet,
son, and come, place your

hand on my skull — your lips
as close as you can to the bone.

Let your words become
particular, let them
strike me

here, above the jaw

and find no

empty space and nothing
broken — no

deficiency between us.

Elisabeth of Schönau (1129–1164) was a German Benedictine abbess who became famous during her lifetime for her prophetic wisdom and ecstatic visions, accounts of which were transcribed by her brother Eckbert. In all, Elisabeth filled three volumes with descriptions of visions that ranged from detailed accounts of visitations from Jesus and Mary to assaults by the devil to admonitions directed at contemporary figures of power. The Catholic Church has remained divided over the value and credibility of Elisabeth of Schönau's visions, and it is unclear how much—or for what purposes—her brother altered and edited her dictations.

O BODY

O body, become a body.

Become a cup, a pen. Become a thing
that can be tipped, and spilled; become

a way of spilling.

O body become a body, become a cup, a pen,
a spilled thing. Become a branch, a rock,
a shallow grave.

Become a bridge, a call.

Oh body, become a voice, and a way of listening.

> As the earth listens to grass growing
> overhead or to graves being dug.

> As a chicken listens to the knife, a shadow
> to a passing cloud.

All night I sat up, wondering. I kept thinking it was quite
simply unbelievable

in light of the history that the body is even

connected to the soul. Or that the soul might
in any way correspond to what the soul is not;

or that what the soul is not might in any way
be permitted to enter or be transmitted by what is,

in light of the history, permitted a soul; or that what is
permitted a soul is,

in light of the history, in any way separate from or
communicable without what has not yet been permitted.

Or that —

                                O body!

                                Divine body!

                                Could it be that
                                after all there is

                                nothing to rejoin?

                                Could it be that,

                                in light of
                                the history of what has

not yet been permitted,

there is no single
truth to pronounce,

only different ways
of speaking?

O!

Brother, hear me. Brother, listen. Brother,
write this down.

Natalya Reshetovskaya (1919–2003) was a Russian chemist, twice married to Aleksandr Solzhenitsyn, who typed the secret manuscripts that would become Solzhenitsyn's many published stories and novels. When, in the name of gathering material for his art, Solzhenitsyn began to conduct extramarital affairs, his relationship with Reshetovskaya deteriorated. In 1970, the two divorced for a second time. Solzhenitsyn married the mathematician Natalya Svetlova and the newlyweds moved to the United States. Soon after, *The Gulag Archipelago* was published to great acclaim. In her memoir, Reshetovskaya wrote that she was "perplexed" by the way that the West accepted her ex-husband's writing as "the solemn, ultimate truth," and argued that its value was, as a result, "wrongly appraised." Despite this criticism and her own subsequent remarriage, Reshetovskaya admitted as late as 2002 that she still loved Solzhenitsyn: "It's possible that it may seem strange and even improper to someone, but, alas, I love him right up to this moment. And the thought never leaves me—will I really never see him again?"

I GO OUT EVERY MORNING

I go out every morning, sometime just after ten. I like to
walk at that hour; it's the familiar rhythm of it, the tip-

tap, tippety-tap of it, that soothes me, that gets me out of
my head.

Of course, they're wild for him now, in America — they
take everything so literally there. They don't know you
can't,

just like that, rub life from one surface to another simply
by pressing it up against a page.

They don't know. The stories went *right through me.*

I can still feel them sometimes: his voice in my ear, my
fingers on the keys.

It's been a long time now since I've written anything down. At least I've stopped wishing I was that other Natalya.

I wouldn't say it was love, now, exactly —

unless everything is love. A way of touching, or wanting to touch upon, what isn't and can never be yours.

In America, see — there's only the future to consider. But over here everything is history — or a way of becoming it.

Sometimes, I dream that my fingers are moving across a keyboard again, only there are no letters on the keys. It's just my fingers and no alphabet — no scroll of paper in the feed. It's just tip-tap, tippety-tap, like the sound shoes make on concrete when they're going somewhere just to turn around and come back again. It's just

words! Just words! Stripped of meaning, literal or otherwise. Stripped even of unspoken things.

"For art's sake," he used to say, in order not to explain.

Well, all right, if life is art. A way of making something from nothing, and then slowly breaking what's been made.

In America, of course, they are wild for him: they believe every single word.

Let them.

The stories went through me, just like they went through that other Natalya. There was no substance to them; nothing to believe in. They filtered through us, like light through leaves.

Simone Weil (1909–1943) was a writer, philosopher, mystic, and political activist whose numerous posthumously published works are marked by both contradiction and clarity. A distinguished scholar, she spent time working in an automobile factory to better understand the effects of industrial labour; a devoted pacifist, she joined an anarchist unit during the Spanish Civil War; a Jewish émigré, she returned to war-torn Europe to work for the French resistance; an unorthodox Marxist committed to social and political revolution, she turned to Occitan poetry as a guide. Weil's spiritual experiences brought her very near to converting to the Catholic faith but, ultimately, she chose to remain outside of the Church and, at every turn, resisted, defied, or subtly overturned dogma and prescription. She died of overwork and malnutrition at the age of thirty-four.

YES, LIKE A POEM. JUTTED UP —

Yes, like a poem. Jutted up — at odds with
but also an extension of the earth.

A form of thought, of breath. Understood

not as a resource to be mined by the body,
also understood as a resource to be mined,

but instead as labour — which is infinite, and
produces nothing.

Yes. A breath. Taken in only to be pressed
out again.

A form of labour, which requires you to

enlist. *To be* enlisted. Which is to say, to

have no choice, be blown. As a speck
of dust is blown

clear across the earth, while at the same
time remaining somehow

a particular body, at odds with it. Yes.

Like a poem. Which requires you

to *be* there — really be there. To jut up.
Stand in the way. To —

without knowing, or needing to know
what the matter is —

be struck by it, as though by a speck of
dust, and recognize the fact of it.

As well as, and as a result, the

contradiction of the body that
reaches past the body in order to

protect itself *against all odds.*

And of the mouth at the centre

that opens to cry,

> "and after me, perhaps,
> a better voice…" more

> inexhaustible, and
> commoner.

Phemonoe, said to be daughter of Apollo, was the inventor of hexameter and the author of the phrase, "Know yourself," which was inscribed above the door to the temple of Apollo at Delphi.

TO FIND A DOOR IS NOT
TO ENTER IT

To find a door is not to enter it: a sign exists only when
read, a line only once it has been measured.

As for existence, it follows its own course, as yet
unlaid. Follow it!

WORKS CITED

Barolini, Teodolinda. "*Paradiso* 1: Con-sort in the Sea with the Other Gods." *Commento Baroliniano*, Digital Dante. May 24, 2023. https://digitaldante.columbia.edu/dante/divine-comedy/paradiso/paradiso-1.

Berger Martinez, Nikki. "Performance Art." Shadow and Growth. August 8, 2023. https://www.shadowandgrowth.com/performance-art.

Carson, Rachel. *Lost Woods: The Discovered Writing of Rachel Carson.* Edited by Linda Lear. Boston: Beacon Press, 1998.

Devi, Shakuntala. *Puzzles to Puzzle You.* New Delhi: Orient Paperbacks, 1976.

Dryden, Edgar. *Melville's Thematics of Form: The Great Art of Telling the Truth.* Baltimore: John Hopkins University Press, 1968, 1999.

Edwards, Sue Bradford and Duchess Harris. *Hidden Human Computers: The Black Women of NASA*. Minneapolis: Essential Library, 2017.

Egan, Margarita. *The Vidas of the Troubadours*. London: Routledge, 1984, 2020.

Heraclitus. *Fragments*. Translated by Brooks Haxton. London: Penguin Classics, 2023.

Higley, Sarah Lynn. *Hildegard of Bingen's Unknown Language: An Edition, Translation, and Discussion*. New York: Palgrave Macmillan, 2007.

Huizinga, Johan. *Homo Ludens: A Study of the Play-Element in Culture*. Eastford: Martino Fine Books, 1955, 2014.

Jando, Dominique. "Annie Frattelini." Circopedia. May 24, 2023. https://tinyurl.com/mve68eak.

Julian of Norwich. *Revelations of Divine Love*. Edited by Barry Windeatt. Oxford: Oxford University Press, 2015.

Kaiman, Jonathan and Justin McCurry. "Papers Prove Japan Forced Women into Second World War Brothels, Says China." *The Guardian*. April 28, 2014. https://tinyurl.com/udcybcfr.

Krönes, Olaf Müller, Roland Schrotthofer, and Florian Weigensamer, directors. *A German Life*. Tel Aviv District, 2016.

Lewis, Paul. "Natalya Reshetovskaya, 84, Is Dead; Solzhenitsyn's Wife Questioned 'Gulag.'" *New York Times*, June 6, 2003. https://tinyurl.com/yyxdczj3.

M.S.R. "A New Documentary Looks at How Roe v Wade Affected Norma McCorvey." *The Economist*, May 26, 2020. https://tinyurl.com/3mth4sjw.

Popova, Maria. "The Poetry of Science and Wonder as an Antidote to Self-Destruction: Rachel Carson's Magnificent 1952 National Book Award Acceptance Speech." *The Marginalian*, November 30, 2022. https://tinyurl.com/48uek8ny.

Sheridan, Michael. "The 'Holy Spirit' Made Her do It: Stenographer Dianne Reidy Offers Godly Excuse for Bizarre House of Representatives Rant." *New York Daily News*, October 18, 2013. https://tinyurl.com/3wvpuahj.

NOTES AND ACKNOWLEDGEMENTS

The cover art is from Nikki Berger Martinez's *Ghost Walk* series, photographed by Riley Salyards. The *Ghost Walk* is an ongoing multidisciplinary art piece combining site-responsive performance art, found object reclamation, costume design, film, and photography. Like other works by Berger Martinez, the *Ghost Walk* suggests that how we relate to matter may be as important as the matter itself.

The costumes for the *Ghost Walk* were created from found materials collected from liminal, abandoned, and forgotten spaces, and each walk emphasizes the vital and necessary connection between the animate and the inanimate, as well as between presence and absence, and between renewal and loss. For Berger Martinez, the process of making art from discarded or otherwise unregarded objects is "to alchemize an imprisoned past into potentiality, fecundity, and freedom." For more on Berger Martinez and the *Ghost Walk* series visit: shadowandgrowth.com.

The quoted material included in the preface on page 10 is from Johan Huizinga's *Homo Ludens*, originally published in Dutch in 1938, with the first English translation published in 1949.

"We Were Taught to Be Seen, Then," takes inspiration from news reports surrounding an event that took place in the United States House of Representatives on October 16, 2013. The poem refers to some details House stenographer Dianne Reidy shared in interviews published immediately following the incident (regarding her early training and skill as a typist), but most — including imagined scenes from Reidy's childhood — are invented.

"Everything Was Still Quite All Right" is comprised almost entirely of adapted quotations from Florian Weigensamer's 2016 documentary feature on the life and career of Joseph Goebbel's personal secretary, Brunhilde Pomsel.

"We Were Computers, Officially" relies on Sue Bradford Edwards and Duchess Harris's 2016 account of an incident in Annie Easley's early career where Easley's image was removed from a group photograph of the Computer Services Division where she worked.

"A Bird Is the Sum of Its Feathers" poses some of the problems included in Shakuntala Devi's 1976 publication, *Puzzles to Puzzle You.*

"I Go Out Every Morning" incorporates the language Natalya Reshetovskaya used to describe her feelings both toward her ex-husband, Alexandr Solzhenitsyn, and his most famous work, *The Gulag Archipelago.* Sourced from various interviews conducted over her lifetime, the comments were compiled in an article published in the *New York Times* directly following her death in 2003.

The quotation included in "Yes, Like a Poem. Jutted Up" is borrowed not from the work of Simone Weil but rather from Dante Alighieri's *Divine Comedy.* As in much of Weil's work, a great theme of Dante's comedy is both the difficulty and urgency of expressing through language — "a medium that is differential and time-bound and linear" (Barolini 2014) — what exceeds representation. In *Paradiso,* the tension between the poet's description of events as he saw them and his simultaneous claim that he will never properly be capable of recounting what he saw, gives rise to the "ineffability topos" Weil grappled with through her thinking, writing, embodied labour, and political resistance.

Heartfelt thanks to my friend Kate Hall who provided detailed feedback and much-needed encouragement during both the early and final stages of this project.

Thank you also to Jessica Moore, Rebecca Silver Slayter, Susan Paddon, Annie Guthrie, and Sam Ace, with whom I shared portions of this manuscript at different times, or discussed its many challenges, and whose friendship, and writing, I cherish.

Thank you to Nikki Berger Martinez and Riley Salyards for generously contributing their work from the *Ghost Walk* series for the cover of this book.

Thank you to Jay and Hazel Millar and everyone at Book*hug for providing a home for this project — as well as a sense of connection to the form of hope Ursula K. LeGuin referred to in her 2014 National Book Award speech. In her speech, LeGuin entreated publishers to value art over profit, and reminded all of us to cherish storytelling not only as one of our oldest forms of freedom but also as a medium through which we expand our collective imagination and, potentially, change the way we live.

Thank you to Carolyn Smart for taking on the role of editor for this book. Given the shared formal and thematic concerns of many of Carolyn's own projects, I knew that I was lucky to have a chance to work with her—but I didn't know how lucky. Carolyn's patience, responsiveness, attention to detail, and depth of understanding of my vision and goals for this collection, have become a vital element within its structure.

Thank you, always, to my family: my parents, Janet and Sandy, the Rosses—Kristin, Scott, Mairi, Lilah, Ollie, James, and Sam—and my kids, Olive and Sol, for their love, and for endless inspiration.

Finally, thank you to my husband, John Melillo, for listening—and listening. As well as for his faith in and support of this project, and all of his generous feedback and ideas about how to think about and experience mediumicity, voice, and sounding, in a world filled with so much difficult and beautiful noise.

Photo: Christine Whelan-Hachey

ABOUT THE AUTHOR

Johanna Skibsrud is the author of three previous collections of poetry, three novels—including the Scotiabank Giller Prize-winning novel, *The Sentimentalists*—and three nonfiction titles, including *The Nothing That Is: Essays on Art, Literature, and Being*, and most recently, *Fool: A Study in Literature and Practice*. An Associate Professor of English Literature at the University of Arizona, Johanna divides her time between Tucson, Arizona, and Cape Breton, Nova Scotia.

COLOPHON

Manufactured as the first edition of
Medium
in the spring of 2024 by Book*hug Press

Edited for the press by Carolyn Smart
Copy-edited by Kaiya Smith Blackburn
Proofread by Laurie Siblock
Design and typesetting by Lind Design
Typeset in Collier
Cover image: Nikki Berger Martinez's *Ghost Walk* series,
photographed by Riley Salyards

Printed in Canada

bookhugpress.ca